CW01501227

CONTENTS

v

I dedicate this book to Olwen Smith to thank her. Without Olwen I would never have got this far. She has been an inspiration to me — and most of all a friend.

I would like to thank all the friends and family that have supported me over the years.

And all my love to my father.

I'd like to dedicate this page to the Manic Street Preachers for inspiring me to fight the waves.

Uncomfortable silences . . .

DIVINE TOOLS

To know they were there was an insurance to myself,
To be glad and hopeful and nothing else,
Because they should have been mine.
Like heaven I waited for my reward,
Dad's divine tools.
To me they were the holy grail,
Of all the things I lost and misplaced,
They were the only things I kept in my sight.
In their golden grace.

Dad would keep them in their pristine condition. If any problems came up, out would come the tools and then the problems would go away. Just like magic, the power of the divine tools. To me they were more than just tools, it was the holy grail after all, but more.

To me they were my dad and everything that I looked up to him about. To me the tools stood for something about his professionalism, being an engineer and being in the RAF for 18 years.

You know I always knew my dad was a professional, the best of the best, and so were his tools, but it's only now I really realise it. I suppose I just took it for granted at that age.

I look back and all I can remember was Dad fixing things, making things and generally doing stuff. So that's what the tools meant to me. More than the outer value.

I remember once when I was young, one time I managed to touch them (it was like getting away with feeling some woman's breast before she noticed) and then my dad shooshing me away.

Even then, when my dad was going through his nervous

breakdown, the only thing that kept me together was the power of the divine tools. Even when I was in care for eight years the power of the force was still strong in me. It was like when Luke said to Obi Wun, 'I can do this.' And that's what kept me going day after day. I would say to myself, 'I can do this! I can do this!' and then know the tools would be in my service one day. But that day never came.

It was a year or two later, when I thought about ringing my family (or what I perceived to be my family at least) that I heard the news. It started when I phoned my mother's father and we were talking about my mum's second marriage. He said she had a church wedding and that's what got me thinking. I said to myself, 'We are Catholics and she has already been married.'

And I said to my grandad, 'How can this be?'

He accused my father of being mentally sick since he was born, making their wedding not real in the eyes of the church. And the first thing that went through my mind was, 'Bollocks! and fucking bastard!' and that it was complete bollocks. They were using my dad as a scapegoat. My dad was not mentally sick as a kid, he became mentally sick in the nineties due to stress and depression over debt (it was called the eighties). My mum's family were just using that as a means of getting a church wedding and make my mum look good in the eyes of the church, they were making her out to be little Miss Saint who married the mental kid. At that point I decided to hang up on my grandad and ring my mum.

We talked, I did not tell her about what I had just heard but I decided to ask her about her wedding. She said she had a church wedding, probably thinking that I would not understand but I understood. I understood oh so well. I decided to hang up. At this point I was really distraught, I think I was the most distraught I had ever been in my life. I was shocked, but the force was still there keeping me together.

So at this point I decided to ring my dad to see how he

was and to see how the divine tools were as well. At this point I decided not to tell my dad that my mum had remarried in church and what it took to do it. All I could think of was, 'Poor man and all of what they said about you. Poor man.' And then I asked him, 'How are you?' He said he was good.

And I said, 'That's good.' I asked him, 'How is the holy grail?'

He said, 'What?'

And I said, 'I'm sorry, I meant your tools.'

He said, 'Oh they got stolen', calm as you like.

I said, 'What! Tell me you're joking.'

He said, 'No.' He said he had to give up his flat.

I said, 'What about your furniture?'

He said, 'I had to leave it behind. I took what I could and what I could put in my room and the rest went into the skip.'

Then I was even more distraught. I replied with the only thing that came into my mind, 'Oh no, Dad.' It wasn't even pain, it was pain of the pain. I tell you I was crying tears as big as Oxo cubes, to think someone would steal this man's tools, what they meant to us and what they stood for to me. 'Poor man,' was my only thought, 'all that we have gone through and now they have gone ... and with it the force that used to be with me.'

The divinity that used to be with the tools has gone too and now they are just stolen property. Now all that I can say is I feel alone as my birthright will not be handed on to me. Typical of life, someone's cheated me out of what should have been. What seems to be the saddest pain to me is that my dad really didn't seem to care at all. I suppose my dad is just not the man he used to be. Life changes people that you used to know, trust me I know. And what can I say now? There will always be a gap that used to be the divine tools.

CIGARETTE TEARS

The commonest form of hiding your emotions.
To never have that moment of weakness.
Just light up and take it all away.
Nobody will ever know or see the emotions
That lie behind that cigarette
Imprisoned in that tarry smoke.
Even though you wonder what it would be like
If they did know, did see your emotions.
But you say to yourself I just can't,
It's not in my nature,
I wasn't brought up to express them,
So I'll have another fag and light up instead.

CLOCKWISE

In darkness lies
Drifting eyes,
A difference not so close.
A voice says
I think before I pose.

Overwind
A reproach mind,
In a clockwork roller coaster
Think, think,
I might, I write,
In darkness light
For one more night.
In darkness lies
Drifting eyes
For a difference, not so close.

CONCEPT

We live in an age of empty promises,
An age when nothing means everything,
And everything means nothing.
Beliefs and ideals are just words,
Instead of the feelings and emotions
That they should be.
Is it just old fashioned to be passionate in beliefs,
Instead of kidding yourself that you belong in this world.
I bring to you a concept.

DEEP IMPRESSIONS

Isn't it funny, the way people look in disgust at me. While I close my eyes and pray to God that I wish I wasn't born.

I think I live in camouflage. Am I transparent? Knowing that I am only one plaster less than a Red Cross parcel. Knowing that I can't spell Red Cross.

Just days, if people ring the bell I freeze, knowing the primal instinct in me, knowing there is a social worker behind the door and seeing my dad barricading it.

CRUCIFIED

Crucified, to never see his eyes,
Crucified, left in the heat that writhed.
As God watched my childhood innocence
Go out the window, without saying a word.
He watched me looking at the devil's pictures,
Without a Lowry in this world.
Crucified, just another person,
Who's had a nail put through his life.

DESIGN AND DELIGHT

Innovation, devastation, designing and delight,
Designing makes magic, four walls and a light.
Perfect innuendos, revelations and their light,
Off to see the architect, bent builders and their like.
Maybe now the financier will go and see the site.
It sounded like a gambler, to put money on the fight.
Innovations, devastations, designing and delight.

DIFFERENT ASPECTS

Sometimes I don't know who I am,
Trapped behind that you-know man.
I wonder how I should be,
With my feelings they don't know me.
Maybe, I am a soulful man.
But behind the scenes,
There are these sinister screams.
I worry that there are two of us,
Trapped together
Like an old umbrella,
That makes me.
That's how it has to be.

A MISDEMEANOUR

A misdemeanour is in my head
When my eyes go red.
Crazy Meg disbelieves my cred,
So I set fire to her head.

A greeting for JAYNE on her birthday, 2000

SUICIDE NOTE

An accident what formed from the evils of sin,
A man who people dislike and punish for being him.
A family what cursed and fights,
From a madman who lies and delights
I am an accident.

DISTANT FATHER

No one left alive,
You said you wouldn't leave me!
All these people lied.
No one left alive.
Death by atomic camouflage,
You have all disappeared.
Well I can't see you!
No one left alive.

I followed your footsteps,
I don't know if I'm near, far or close,
I see there's no light, no tunnels,
No, no nothing.
No life.
Just me.
God forgive me Father,
I want to go home.
I want to be a part of it all.
Forgive me.

DOWNWARDS CASCADE

We live when there is no point in living,
We become corrupted when there is no evil,
We talk when we should be thinking,
We don't think when we stare at the clouds,
We embrace when there is no one to be embraced,
We love but there is no one to be loved,
We cry but there are no tears,
We say we are faithful but we lie,
There is no truth.

A BROTHER'S LOVE

Would you saw into me?
Take my pain away?
Would you take me apart?
And leave me to bleed from the heart?
Saw my limbs off,
And say it is harsh?

You lead me up this deadly path,
No, no, you are my brother.
But I said I'm not heavy.
You said it didn't matter.
This blood does not make us the same.
You are going to take the pain.
You are going to take me apart.

Would you kill me and say it's so?
Would you take my hands from my soul?
Just listen to these tragic cries.
This bitter sickness makes me cry.
Does it make you a killer by my side?

A WOMAN'S FAKE LAUGH

Is it romantic to die?
For a moment there I lost myself,
But I came back,
For the retrospect of life.
It was almost lovely to die,
Nearly gay but that's just life.
With Brittany's tits in my eyes,
And life and lust and lies.
A righteous man said I was sick.
Staring in the corner
With this deep breath sigh.
My my.
With my fascination for death,
Loneliness and pain.
Just to die, a freedom of sense.
I lost myself.
But the trouble is I came back.

AARON

A soulful rain showers us.
We can only see black and white,
And not the colours that are bright.
It keeps me awake.
I worry about this.
I wonder if there is anything
We could have done, or do,
Anyone we could have saved.
I think to myself, 'Why are we like this?
We would rather watch somebody suffer
Than to show them love, God help us!'
I don't think I can carry on like this,
In this soulful rain.

AKA PURIFICATION

I am on my knees trying to pray
You exist when there is trouble!
I say your name,
Jesus Christ,
God forgive me.
Hail Mary,
Our Father,
Elaborate device.
A walking touché,
Just save the day.
My mother died yesterday,
My father died on Thursday,
And today is my day.
Genocide day.
Time to believe, one last time,
Jesus Christ, please help me
Or I will die.

ALL BUT DIFFERENT NOW

We live our lives in fear,
That's what they say, don't they?
Silly, really, fear!
The one thing that people can't take away from us.
Do you ever notice how we stare at people,
And wonder what that person's like?
I do all the time.
It's like when a person changes
And they become all but different in many ways.
Like life we are led in different directions.
I remember that moment of thought,
Which started the conversation.

AM I REALLY ME – DEEP PAIN

Why what does it matter?
What does it mean to you?
You don't believe in me,
You don't miss me.

Always this feeling of love.
You don't believe in love.
You watched me go past,
You didn't say.

You hated that I came from you.
You make me pay.
You pretended that you liked me,
And pushed me away.

You make me feel hate,
Why did you do it?
Why didn't you care?
Why don't you care?

Are you so vain
You didn't know?
Am I not who you thought I was?
Do you only love yourself?

Who am I today?
Who am I?
I miss the thought of love.
Why did you run away?

I always think of love.
Why did you run away?
Who am I today? I don't know.
You make me miss the feel of love.

I am always tearful, just to pray.
Always this feeling of love.
This torture shouldn't have been for me.
Does it seem fair to you?

BEAUTIFUL OLWEN

Still trying to find the time.
You work too hard,
And that's just the start.
No lies they ask too much from you.
You always give in.
No prima donnas here!
You'll stay to the bitter end.

Hours don't mean a thing to you.
You'll help and help until you go blue.
That seems silly to me,
But that's just my point of view.
And that cat has done a poo!

You've got to slow down,
Make it easy on yourself.
It you carry on like this,
Your hair will fall out.
And I haven't got a doubt about it.

BEING DAD

One of the first memories I have is the picture of looking up
    to my dad and holding his hand.
And that was the most defining moment of my life.
And that memory has stuck with me ever since.
And now all I can long for is to be Dad.
To get back to that memory.
To be in that father and son relationship.
To be in that loving family.
Something since the age of ten that has got more special every
    year that passes.

BETWEEN

I can't see.
Alone.
Crying for help.
Sad but still alive.
I don't want your help.
I've got plan B,
It helps me
Survive.
I don't want to be you,
My standards
Are not that high.
Just cry, lying doubt,
F-word shout.
Not knowing,
Knowing,
Calling,
Yeh leave a message.
'Hi it's me again,' doubt.
Aberrent, aberrent, F-word shout.
It's all regret, not knowing.
'It's not so bad,' I said,
Lying to my doubt.

What was if only if you could never forget

BORN USELESS AND UNFORGIVEN

Born useless and unforgiven
THEY CRY.
Tears of sanity
    Hoping to be insane.

Free us from this
        Free me
            I am the plague
        The plague of the plague
                FOR
            Whoever I touch will be damned.

And I am sorry for it
Please, PLEASE set me on fire
Because I have no home.

CANNED FRUIT

Such is life
    Forbidden fruit,
Such are lies
        Lie in peace
                Untouched by lice.
                Untouched by LIFE.
            LIES DENY FRUIT PEACH BREASTS.
Sweet lies of life
    Temptations mess
            Adulterous arrest
        Intruding.
            Bless
                Immaculate conception
                Not a bastard's face in breasts.

Smothered in bacon and red sauce
    Sainsbury's fed
    Coughing up white wine
    To remove the red of Marlborough's best
                Swine of swine
                The herd
                        Shepherd
                        Lord
                        The rest.

BRITISH RULES

Do not doubt yourself,
I am working class.
Meaning by this – I work for a living,
With the rest of Great Britain.
I am English
I am British
I am united with my Scotsmen and Welshmen,
Don't forget the Irish too.

I am not saying it's not hard
But I was brought up by the British rules.
Fair play, honesty, compassion,
Home pride, innocence,
As a God-loving Christian.
By this we can overcome anything.

I am not institutionalised
I am just living.
Forget me not.
I am not being racist by this.
I am ethnic,
I am Asian and Jewish,
We are all British in heart.

CALL FOR A REPAIR MAN

There is a broken record player in my head,
Stopping, starting, never giving me a rest.
It's hard to live with this broken mess.
Living with this rewinding pest.
It's always picking on me,
Probably because of someone I used to be.
Trapped in this clattered mess,
Waiting for the repairman.

A BACK OF THE HOUSE MONSTER

There is a monster in the back of our house,
Left there like a half-used appliance,
Looking for a new home.
He's not allowed to come round the front.
After all he is a monster!
Trapped in this patio doom.
Always nimble in his expressions,
Knowing he shouldn't really be here.
But he is.
And he's already scaring next door's cat.
What do you do with a back of the house monster?
I don't know, maybe we should ask Pat.

A DIFFERENT MADNESS

Would you find that you have gone
And your nights do not belong?
To see with different eyes,
That's why you are different,
Surprise.

I do not know what to say,
You were once the greatest man I knew.
And now you're different.
I'm blue.

These problems have caught up with you.
I didn't think they would but they did.
You knew.

All that we had has gone.
All that we know is different.
Maybe for the worse,
Maybe for the good,
It's just a shame.
I cried and I think I made it worse.

A LAST-MINUTE TEAR

A preference to life is nice,
Beautiful, but no disguises.
Just like ice.
Cool, refreshing but blinding.
No lies, just delights, that's life,
Nice.
My epiphany.

WE'VE GOT A MAN DOWN

War is sore on blisters,
Itching, scratching, sore,
Attacking, war.
Unliberating, lingering,
Attacking, sore,
Unmatching, raw,
Unknowing, unseeing,
Isolated, dead.
No more, no more.

A MERE REFLECTION OF MYSELF

Is this me?
I have a doubt.
I can't see my eyes.
Just in time for a black-out.
I look at myself,
I see Hyde but I can't see Jekyll.
Is this me?
Why?

Why does my body lie?
I pity this fool who is this person.
Oh shit – it's me.
Just a bitter unreliability.
Mirrors forgive me
Because I put myself on to you.
Damn this uncanny sham.
I lie here stricken.
Me. Me. Me.
Just to be me.
I am here inside but not outside.

Written from my dark side on my birthday

A PRAYER FOR OLWEN'S BIRTHDAY

I am your son.
You are my ever-loving Lord.
I wait for you
And live in your grace.
You are, the best of light
The divine light.
I follow you in your wellbeing,
Knowing never-ending love and warmth,
That welcome me into your kingdom.

A SEVEN-DAY LIFE

The end awaits,
So many memories I picked up on the way.
The lights of the city,
The crazy rain,
The sun, blue,
And distant friends.
So many memories, I take to my grave.
Laughing in the mornings,
Tears on a Sunday afternoon.
So many memories overwhelm me,
Life's gone too soon.
As I rest for the end,
The end waits for me,
Life pleasured me.

A TABLE-TOP PROSTITUTE

Table-top prostitute,
A slave to cleanliness.
Wiping away all of humanity's nastiness.
Used by pricks and ignorant people,
Who are dying in their own excrement.
And then she sorts them out,
They leave smelling of roses,
Another day's work done.
But at the end of it she knows,
That the ignorant pricks will be back – the next day.

THOMAS THE TWIN

Thomas – will you die with me?
I who was born to make peace with the bees.
Thomas who was always by my side,
Never doubting, never minding what people say.
Faithfullest of friends,
You, me and Peter always binding us three.
Thomas the twin – look at him and you will see me.
That's how it was meant to be,
The reflection of our father.
Relieves me to see the twin Thomas,
The man who befriended me.

UNIVERSE

On a sea of nothing feelings are forming around the world,
Love is formed into existence, miracles happen.
I said yes, I know!

Darkness is not so dark now,
Brightness to my eyes,
I am home.

On a sea of nothing darkness flows through the universal soul.
One feeling started life, forever creating,
You will never know.

VENTING SPLEEN

I saw in your eyes that you hate the world,
Pleasant to know someone does,
I hate it too.
A fire rages between us,
We rule the world in our fury.
We cleared the canopy, the outlook.

We found our inner selves,
Peace, harmony,
Midriff bellies sigh.

WE LOVED YOU BUT YOU NEVER KNEW

The unforgettable love a missing friend.
Some people won't believe in heaven,
But, I kind of believe in heaven,
As a memory of the happiest time in your life
Being lived, over and over,
As a continuing dream of joy.
An unforgettable being of your life,
That never stops, that never ends.
In this you know,
That God is looking over time,
With a continuous wink,
That praise in our Lord and the dreaming begins.

WHAT FEELINGS WE HAVE

What feelings we keep down our heads,
Downer, downer, past our necks.
But once or twice these feelings come up,
Reminds us of emotions that we threw up.
Only if you say these names,
Byron, Blake and Dylan Thomas,
Emotion of poetry comes out of my veins,
For a minute or two I embrace them through.
Left with these melancholic moods
And a worry about what the next day brings.
What feelings we have.

WHAT IS TIME IF YOU HAVE TO KILL
THE SUBLIME?

I am unity, without giving my soul away,
I am discipline, without showing you the game I play.
You and me, we are the fury that woke the beginning.
You know I play victim to the system that brought us
    together.
Only from this I know what love is and that it is sound.
I might just be proud of that, I just might.
The system that led us together, for ever and ever and more.
The sublime.

WHAT WOULD IT TAKE TO MAKE ME HAPPY?

I should imagine that would be on my gravestone.
I think of all the things that could make me happy, maybe.
An Italian wife, fast cars, lots of money, a house in the
    country.
But at the end of the day, I don't think anything could.
I think I'm beyond happiness.
It's not in my DNA.
As the Manics said, 'DNA means does not accept.'
And that's me.

WINDOWS OF MADNESS

What are you looking at Dad?
There's nothing there Dad – come away.
What are you looking at Dad?
Please don't tell me you're going mad.
Please don't look through it Dad
They'll send you away!
You're looking through those windows again.
Oh bloody hell Dad,
And you're saying Jesus is under the stairs,
And Santa Claus is in the fridge.
Please come away.
I'll make those windows pay,
Double glazing go away.
Go away.
Leave my dad alone.

YOU CANNIBAL

The meat raw stains of nicotine blood,
Raw pubescent lung,
Kidney failed sin of Herbert's son.
Pickled fresh,
Having it funny
You know it's best.
Pity me pitta bread,
Side plate of relish
Absolutely ravished Fred.
Yes I am who I am,
Raw fresh miser,
Who loves subtle flesh.

WILD LOVE

Hope and praise, hope and praise,
For you my love, hope and praise.
Wild blackberries and snow, and playful tiptoes.
Hope and praise, hope and praise,
For me my love, hope and praise.

SILENT ROOM

So quiet, not a sound to be heard.
Silent room, where is the life that used to belong in you?
Where is the beauty that used to shine through you?
How can this be? That you are alone?
Where is her laughter that belonged with you?
Empty, alone.
There are only tear drops in you now.
Silent room

From what love found in heaven is yours.
Dedicated to my Nan, Nell.

SOCIETY'S MACHINES

Dispensing everlasting gratification,
Faceless, with a receipt to hand,
Always biding their time,
They are always in line.
Left with puritans, laughing at their hand.
Unresponsive in feelings,
Knowing they are going to be hanged for society's use,
Damned of the damned,
Left weeping inside,
Never knowing what's outside,
Trapped in these four corners,
One exit blocked by hands,
Stubborn in use,
Only one more thing to say,
'How can I help you?'
That's what I have to say!
Society's used.

STRAWBERRY FEELINGS

Glossy pages waiting to be looked at,
Pages of inspiration felt warm to the touch.
Outstanding beauty pleading for attention.
Strawberry feeling exploding,
Before the pages' touch.

Images of something perfect that you love,
And would it be wrong to say that you do?
But some things warm and tender, that you lust.
Or is it that something missing,
Would cause a dream of sudden collapse?
That, they call love.

OAP

As the old become beautiful, feeble and liars
Dante's tribe circling the world,
Locked in hands like old false teeth polygrip tight.
As they say their special words, inspiring words,
Like 'Everest' and 'Titanic at night'
Peaceful moments, yawnful times,
Special old people, special old lives.

FOOTSTEPS

Hardness breaks on true believers,
Many such as I that lay down their lives for peace,
Memories keep us going,
Memories are our being,
Such as souls,
Not know one true thing but many.
Devils point, angels sing,
I can only hope with a tear in my heart,
For love, for life, for sorrow and me.

3D

The drip, drip dripping
Patters through my soul,
An open tap left to flow.
Life slowed, it said hello,
I wondered who I was,
The water flowed,
I remembered.
I said goodbye
Because I am
The maintenance man.

I CAN'T LIVE LIKE THIS AFTER
WATCHING TV

In every day, in every way,
Doing a nine to five job.
Clinging to nothing,
Hoping for fame.
Contrast, beauty of television
And ugliness of life.
How can I live like this
After watching TV.

TV promotes everything,
God and universe in one.
Infatuation with television
Imparts a message to me,
And at least I try and pretend to live my life
In this world, this universe, this TV.

THE MANICS, YOU HAVE ALWAYS BEEN THERE, MY DEDICATION

Like the brothers I have always looked up to,
The brothers I never had.
While I was trapped in this deep hole, thrown back so far,
They were the only people to bring me back.
Like heaven up above, they called.
They said, 'What tears fall from this great height?'
While I looked up and saw this bright light,
And then knew the Manics would always be there.
Even if they weren't,
They would be in my heart and in my mind,
Keeping me going, ticking, surviving.
Always everlasting.
That's what the Manics mean to me.
Their music, their beliefs, the concept.
All because of the brothers I looked up to,
The Manics.

TEMPLATE

Goddamned little boy,
Suddenly so fine,
Sing like you just don't want to sing.
Take it into your mind that I watched you,
Processing information.
Don't deny yourself a little bit of joy.
Appreciation fine; suddenly so.
From a packet of ribs you were born,
It burns.

THE DTS

I am losing the war,
Queuing to see Lucifer.
If hate makes betrayal,
Then life makes sense,
And the devil will repent.
I give them the respect they deserve.
Chains tearing my soul.
Thousands of soldiers to go.
I dream of flowers,
I say no more.
We die as killers,
As killers we die.

THE LAST MAN STANDING – RECYCLING DIGNITY

As the generation uproar begins bridging the gap,
As the young become old and the old become no more,
We whisper to each other,
'The last man standing, the last man standing.'
While laughing at our faces,
And waiting to become no more,
We watch the grey affect our being,
And bend over our legs from the strain of laughing.
Some people call it madness,
But I call it being competitive.
While always remembering the rules.
Rule number one – the last man standing.
Rule number fifty-two – the last man standing.

And then it becomes me,
Like my forefathers, I am the last man standing,
And the young become old,
And I become no more.

THE PROPHET

No, I don't know my place,
And of course you'd be the one to tell me!
I see random DNA copying itself,
And then come back to show me.
It listens and clones,
Aspires to intelligence,
I see double cyclones,
Two twists of anger
Attacking me.
I am worried, scared,
Laughing to make sure I'm not dead,
Paranoia shakes me,
Makes me believe in weird things.
Am I dreaming?
This can't be real,
Make it nil nil for me,
I must be hallucinating.

THIS STAR OF OURS

Imagine looking at this star,
And then seeing it explode right in front of your eyes.
And then realise,
This star died millions and millions of years ago.
And now what you are seeing is the reflection of the past,
Catching up with you with a glittering sigh.

How can you justify anything now?
This star of ours said goodbye.

ONE LESS LONELY MAN

Loneliness curves around the road,
Breaking, swerving, stopping.
Loneliness *purves* around you go.
Red lights are all thrown in.
Loneliness hurts,
Yes you know.
Tears falling,
Off the cliff you go.
One less lonely man,
But nobody knows.

OPEN

Sometimes I wonder if the open road calls me,
The lights of the cities,
The lights of the stars,
Approach me.

Open land,
Sky that never ends,
Simple thoughts of life,
Appreciation that remains with me.

PEEPING TOMALINA

You run in the shadows,
Hiding away,
I know you're there,
Say, we can play.
Your eyes call me over,
Always smiling at me.
I wonder what you're thinking,
Maybe it's of me.

You are silent and sweet,
You don't speak to me.
Maybe I'm dreaming,
Just you and me.

You run in the shadows
Hiding away,
I know you are there,
Say, we can play.

You're always smiling,
You don't tell me things,
Your eyes call me over.
I wonder what you're thinking.
Maybe it's sins.

POIGNANT

Man's biggest enemy is himself,
With a knife in one hand and a holy book in the other.
Preaching compassion, while prostituting his fellow man.
Isolated and callow, saying death is the only way out.
Oh so true, maybe.
Being complacent, pointing the blame at someone else.
Staring at paintings, identifying the colours,
Seeing the picture, just maybe.

PROBABLY BOY

Born one in every million,
We know each other by that feeling.
Something not right but unquestionable,
Just believing.
Melancholic minds, a slave to feeling.
Yes, producing art.
Art dealers come over for the weekends.
Thoughts become many,
Dealing with institutionalised people.
Heartbroken, tired.
Questioning your own work,
Forever in a queue.
Tears of happiness,
Waiting for your next review.
Yes my boy, I know you.

PROTECTED BY THE GOVERNMENT
– IN CARE

Death and pain comes for you,
You wonder what to do,
What to do at all.
Hail, braille and hell come for you.
They shatter your soul,
It's gone down the loo.
What to do at all.
Tears and treacle make fun of you,
Left at a papier mâché zoo,
You don't know what to do,
What to do at all.
At half past two,
You kill yourself.
You are only thirteen,
Nobody knew,
Nobody knew you at all.
Death is honest
Strangely alive,
Peaceful now.

RAINBOW

Doubting Blue,
How did you know that I love you?
Did Whispering Red tell you?
Or was it Orange or Pink?
Yes it must have been Feminine Pink.
Or was it Outrageous Orange?
Please tell me Doubting Blue.
So my love my secret's out,
I so wish I could have told you first.
But after all like my colour, I am Yellow.
All my friends told you first,
My colours, my love, Blue.

Inspired by Charles Dobson

RUBBISH, YOU IDIOT

Once used always forgotten,
Never to see the light again.
Trapped in this rotten mess.
Why didn't you recycle me, you pest?
So dirty and misplaced,
Lingering with fingerprints,
What a dirty waste.
And it's always never your fault,
You threw me out, without one.
Are you brain-dead or something?
Try putting me in the blue or red box
And next time, I will say toodly pip
Instead of all this rot.

SELFISH

My problems are more important than yours!
That's how the world works.
That's how he thinks the world works.
But not.

How deluded are you.
To say selfish would be nasty but true.
You mess us about and all we want to do is help you.
How could you?
You won't even help yourself.
And it's like putting a knife through our sides,
Watching you kill yourself.
All the time you give us that look,
Of the unwritten law – of being proud.
What crap!
Look where being proud got you.
Now you are dying and we haven't got time to meet you.
How selfish.

SHYNESS

Shyness is a terror that invades my system,
A terrorist from within that never leaves me alone.
That isolates me from other people that I would love to
    meet.
All I am left with is these aberrant moods.
Forever alone and distraught.
A sentence for life with a soft name called shyness.

BLOODY TEARS

Life that once seemed so precious,
Seems in disarray, in beliefs and colours.
As one soldier falls down, another soldier stands up.
And the game begins again.
Bloody tears.

I SEE ALONE

Is life truly right or wrong,
And nothing in the middle?
Because that's where I lie.
Not right, but not mental.
Say a higher point of directions.
That's where I am.
But if I could be the same level
As everybody else
Then that part that makes me would be dead.
And would that be a love missed?
The unaware attraction that makes me.
Maybe it's good not to be right.

INSTITUTIONALISED NATURE

Soap smells like stability,
Just a trademark that keeps you the way you are,
A shallow comforting that never says goodnight.
Reminds me of childhood,
Smiling, Dreaming, Family, Lego
And the like.

Soap's a wonder,
That we never talk about.
A missing link between us, and the people we don't want to
    be.
More used than religion, our saviour to be.
We live up to you Tesco's home brand.
May God be in you,
You'll never walk away,
Soft and squidgy just to play.

ISN'T IT WONDERFUL

Isn't it wonderful.
You are young and sweet,
Your dark eyes glisten at me,
And that's neat.

You have a radiant smile,
And you are just petite.
I wish I knew you.
Just to touch you,
That would be great.
Just to know you like me.

I think intimate thoughts,
They are there.
I wonder what to do next.
It's just amazing.
I think to myself, 'Oh wow!'

But the bus is stopping.
I've got to say something now.
She says she's only fifteen,
And I think 'Damn!'
'Do you want to go to the pictures then?'

JUST THE WAY IT IS

Maybe if I never hope for much, life will be OK.
Maybe if I never hope for much, life will be OK.
Dying of sympathies, of regret,
Left and upset, left alone and unknown,
Maybe it's just regret.
Maybe if my friends said my name,
Life wouldn't be a pain.
Maybe if I'd never hoped for much, life would be OK.
I just stopped to say these words, just the way it is.

LEFT ALONE LIKE TEARS TO STONES

Here I am trapped in my mind,
Criticism, say I'm blind.
They point and stare and deny I'm here.
Left to die
While they deny.

They string me up,
And take my belief and make it disbelief.
I said I can help you.
While they deny the denies.
I came to help.
My father will save you.

They say I shouldn't be alive.
I haven't got a right to live.
They pierce me with nails,
And say I do not know what pain is.

While I am hanging
My blood is dripping.
My mother is ripped away from me.
From a hand of a Roman.
I call for you Father,
I call for you.
The children deny me Father.
Help, help me.
Peter, where are you?
Left alone like tears to stones.
Now I come to you Father.

MIXED VIEWS

To never know where you have come from,
This is the greatest lie that you have said.
What are you on?
What did you say?
Rabies and pain.
Don't make it sound the same.
Just go – stop messing about.
Don't tell me, your laugh throws me out.
What are you on?
I see northern lights.
Are we in your shed?
Bugger me – you're right.
Can this be, that you make sense to me?
Can this be?
Can this be? That you make sense to me.
Can this be?
Someone open the window please.
Can this be, that you make sense to me.

MY CHILDHOOD

I remember hiding under the stairs, telling myself 'I'm all alone and no one loves me and I can't read or write'. I look back, I find that's not bad for the age of seven, I wouldn't like to know what I was like on a bad day.

Remembering what it was like at school. I could not catch up in my special class. Even with kids in the same boat I was last in the queue. Mrs Corbett was so angry with me in class. I think I found it hard to think at that time, knowing I was alone. At the same time I remember being bullied, probably because I was last of the last.

My dad was a distraught man and we were very poor. We had no money. I did not have much, I had the same clothes every year. That's probably why I was picked on. I just remember people having the new Reeboks every year and I just had the same stuff. It doesn't help having a single parent.

I remember that one time Sarah Garden called me a tramp to my face. I was sitting down by Mrs Corbett but she didn't do anything about it. My thoughts at the time, 'I suppose that's what it means to be poor or different, am I Jewish or Welsh?' I used to watch a lot of World War Two films and Colditz. I was very clever at a young age, I knew I wasn't going to be a rocket scientist but I knew the game, I knew what's what. The really annoying thing about it was that she thought it was funny. She looked at me and just smiled. I was looking up to the teacher, I was expecting justice but she must have thought there was some sort of truth to it, I was labelled.

Oh well life goes on.

Oh no, Dad's mainly sick now, I have to spend eight years in care. Oh crap.

MY GUILT FOR TAKING A BROTHER
OR SISTER'S LIFE

I sleep in sadness because of the way fate mocks me
With the thousands of choices of persons,
Which could have been me, but not.
I was the second born in my family and the last child.
And if I was trying to describe myself I'd probably say,
'I am a slave to guilt.'
Guilt has always been with me, or maybe it's just disgust.
Disgust with myself.
I would rather miss the brother or sister that could have
    been me,
Than justify my life.
I think of the person that could have been here,
And feel so sorry, for taking his or her go.
I just think of what beauty could have been here,
Instead of myself.

NOT NOW

Born in dismissal.
Unwanted cries fill the room.
Lonely faces pass the window.
Forgotten games left in a cupboard
Never to be seen again.
Kids point and laugh,
They talk,
'You don't know your mum'
'You don't have a mum.'
I run,
Crying in the corner.
Feel better afterwards
Go to Dad.
Expect warmth,
Dad looks away from me,
Head in hands.
I don't know what to say.
Feel alone.
Jump.
Off stairs.
One by one.
I jump
Gearing up for the big day.
But that's later – in the future.
Go under the stairs and sit.
Write on the wall,
Don't want to be in this family,
I don't want to be me.

NOT SO TRUE LOVE

My redemption of laughter,
Laughter of love,
Taken away from me.
Shallow tears, not forsake me.
Maybe just pity,
Pity that overwhelms me.
I cannot go back now.
Death welcomes me.
Together, not so true love.
Together.

FORGIVEN HELL

Scene 1
Forgiven hell, open doors.
'They say death fears us.'
Found this soul, born from nothing.
'You've been given love,
Your debts paid,
Move on, move on,' they say.
'You believe in love don't you?'
'No I don't, shame.'

Scene 2
Introduced into society,
'Love is hell,' just another brave face.
'Who am I where do I come from?
These are my questions.'
No, no answers here,
They just shout out for help.
Inflictions of pain.
They've been given love.
'No way out, I hear their screams.
We are being punished.
They tell me to accept their love
After every teardrop.'
Love is all around.
'I want to go back.
Fire, flames, tortured back,
I want to go back.'

Scene 3
Love through tears,
'Help, all this fear of love.
Help, I believe in love.'

F-WORD CRYPTIC

You don't really matter, that's what they tell me,
That's what they always tell me.
Day after day they will say it.
Tantalise it, linger it, rub it in my face.
Smoke it in their pipe and say have a nice day.
F-word cryptic I would say.
Everyone I'd see would say it to me,
Social workers, foster families,
Even people beside me when going for a pee.
Statistics they pointed at me.
I would say if I didn't really matter,
Why do you always say it to me?
F-word cryptic I would say.
They just say you have to pay, you have to pay.

GLASSHOUSE BIG BROTHER

I can only hope or wonder.
What am I going to do
              Or not do?

Popularity is a flavour that doesn't last long in the public's mouth.

With this in mind
I will take my opportunity for FAME.
I WANT TO LIVE FOR EVER.

As they say there are only a few opportunities
                              for happiness in life
                                    And I will take them all
                                    And be judged for it
                                    For all to see.

I am their rag doll

I WANT TO LEARN HOW TO FLY

GLENFORD

A continuing person who catches light,
Praising the things that come before him.
Not saddened by the darkness but profound,
With a smile for life.
Yes my boy you have life and I, who died of cancer.

FRAGMENTS

God saw me in the corner,
Saw my eyes glistening in the dark,
Brought me forward to the light.
My eyes were open
Once more I could breathe.

I will look for you past destiny and sight,
Breaking my mind,
Answering my life,
Through darkness I lie.

Sunny old town, and a sunny place to be,
When you break the past,
We'll find it hard to leave,
Summer times go so fast,
We didn't have time to pray.

Summer time loving past to be,
Summer old town to see.

HAVE A GREAT SUMMER

They surround us, devils lubricated in their fake masks.
They come from all four corners saying there is no animosity
As I anticipate their punches.
The other lost souls turn their backs on me
With high-pitched screams.
What can I say Mum, have a great summer.
This classic line always comes back to me.

HUNGRY CAT

There you are cat, meowing in my ear,
Don't tell me you're hungry,
You haven't disappeared.
I fed you less than half an hour ago,
But that was then and this is now,
Is that what you're trying to tell me in your meow?
Is that why you are running around my legs
And saying I'm not really a pest?
No, cat, you're a pet but not a pest.
There you are cat, meowing in my ear.

I ASKED FOR HELP BUT I NEVER GOT IT

For years of years of asking for help,
Always saying please, always getting hurt,
Always in a sad frame of mind.
Never seeing the light, always over my mind.
Asking for help but never to get it.
Left in a corner, shy,
Wondering if anyone would notice me on their way by.
Asking, asking, should I even need to?
Am I invisible or have I died?
As I realised that asking for help, sucks.
And I will carry on with this sad frame of mind.

I CAN NEVER BRING YOU BACK

People ask me how do you cope with it?
I don't know I tell them, life goes on I suppose.
For the first few years it was hard,
You know that feeling of terror?
Well I got that every day.
I know that feeling.
I'm sure it never meant to cause any trouble.
But it did.
It was there for a reason,
But I didn't understand what that reason was for.
I was always a daddy's boy,
And my dad was the greatest man I knew,
He was my star in the sky,
It broke my heart when he became ill.
For the first three months while I was in care,
I thought he would get better
And I would be able to go home.
But after the first year,
I knew it wasn't happening,
And I was stuck in the system,
Or as I called it, the mud.
Now looking back,
I know what that feeling of terror meant,
It was the fear of losing my dad.
Something I never got over even to this day.

I PLAY THE ANGRY MAN

Post-modern poetry,
Stereotypical if you ask me.
Lying because of a bloodclot,
Telling you things that you already know.
Devils in pinstripes,
Giving you quotes for you to say, 'Oh no!'
Libyan terrorists come knocking at your door,
Saying 'Is that one pint or two?'
'Get away you bastards,
I don't want no yoghurt off of you!'
Post-modern poetry.

THE FAITHFUL FEW

We who have conscience will walk
To the farthest points of our knowledge
And cross hands.
We will guide travellers and sing them songs.
That was our dream.
I'm the last one now.

We were pure in our thoughts
But knowledge was dangerous in our minds.
Our one conscience became individual.
We struck each other,
We killed the travellers,
Our temples became weapons,
Our grace became fury.
I'm the last one now.

I used God's name to quiet my friends,
I am red-handed, the blood will never come off.
Every thing I set out to do I betrayed.
I will take my life in horror of myself,
Uttering Judas,
And wake up in hell as I expected.
We who have conscience will walk
To the farthest points of our knowledge and cross hands.

LOST AND FOUND

Sigh for me and I'll sigh for you.
Long live the runaway town.
Old-living souls, lost and then found,
Singing old songs that sounded sound.
That's where I want to be,
Lost and then found.

HOTEL TO HOTEL

How humble I can be if you will let me be.
How peaceful I can be if you sing to me.
How loving I will be if you open the door to me.
How perfect I would be for you,
If you came back to me.
My darling I miss you.

NO ONE KNOWS ME – I DON'T EVEN KNOW ME – WHO'S WHO

You say that you know me but you don't,
My thoughts are my thoughts,
My own private world.
You say that you know me but you don't.
You don't know me.
You don't know me.

You don't know what lies behind here,
So leave it alone.
You might be afraid of what you can see.
Cruelty and torture is not yet deceased,
They could come back
And face you with your disbelief.

You don't know me.
You don't know me,
So leave me alone,
And you won't go wrong.
You say that you know me but you really don't,
You don't know me so leave it alone.

WORKING-CLASS KID MAKES GOOD

So you think I'm stupid,
But you don't know me.
You treat me like a sin.
Maybe that's the person you want to see,
But it's not me.

I want to get out of here and make it big.
To live my life.
What would life mean to me?
What would it be – to be?
This is for me to see.
And I will see.

With hope and glory in my eyes,
I will go.
I will not be hypnotised,
Into being someone I am not.
You will see me in the stars,
And know I have not forgotten you.

THE DANIELS

Jackie Jack never right,
Not until I've had you all night.
Dreams of black, dreams of blue,
I find I've been kicked in,
By the rubbish compact,
Because of the inspirations of Jack.
Left on the floor with a shattered smile,
Picked up by a blond bombshell,
That's how Jack came right.
Just one of these nights.
That's how.

OUR MINDS, OUR SOULS

Can man and woman make beauty,
That we can perceive and not know of it?
Is that why we take our lives so easily,
And do not stick around to look at it?
Because we do.
We do make beauty,
And we do not spend the time to look at it.
We should open our minds and take in the sights.
Our minds, our souls, praise the things that we love.
That's the meaning of life,
We have been given it.
So make beauty.

INNER MIX

As a country of nations linked to immigration,
Beautiful poses, only because you're different,
As different as the next person.
All framed neatly in a line,
But not forced to be kind.
The identity's not right,
But a remixed population outfight.
Home Office predicts no tender lies,
But you might think the British might disguise,
But not.
As found the beauteous flowers come,
From all different properties.
As this nation sleeps in peace.

Dedicated to the Bradford riots

GATES OF HEAVEN

He turned from the gates of heaven, why?
He said to me, 'We are all influenced by each other.'
He wanted to give back to me what I gave to him.
'Fair enough,' I said, fair enough, 'I applaud you.'

I would be very happy to hear any comments about my work. Please email to: stchris_uk@yahoo.co.uk

Chris Harper

First published in Great Britain in 2004 by
The Book Guild Ltd
25 High Street
Lewes, East Sussex
BN7 2LU

Typesetting in Bembo by
Keyboard Services, Luton, Bedfordshire

Printed in Great Britain by
Antony Rowe Ltd, Chippenham, Wiltshire

A catalogue record for this book is available from
The British Library

ISBN 1 85776 783 7

A ROSE BY ANY OTHER NAME IS A TREE

Christopher K Harper

The Book Guild Ltd
Sussex, England

A ROSE BY ANY OTHER
NAME IS A TREE